Kate Melton

Tom's Great-Grandma Eileen

Helping Children
to Understand Death,
Grief and Loss

"Who's in that photo?" said Tom with a frown,
"The one on the wall that you never take down?"

"Proudly displayed for each person to see,
It just makes me wonder – whoever is she!?"

"That is Eileen, my grandmother," said Mom,
"Always so gracious and always so calm."

"She made up great stories of fairies and knights,
Her cakes were so scrumptious, I loved every bite!"

"The most loving grandma that ever had been."
"Then, let's go and see her!" said Tom, looking keen.

"I'm sorry, my dear, but that we can't do.
She died when I was a bit older than you."

"Died?" replied Tom, "But, what does it mean? Why can't I meet my great-grandma Eileen?"

"You see," replied Mom with a long wistful sigh,
"Everyone's born, then we live, then we die."

It's the cycle of life to which we belong.
But luckily, her life had been fun-filled and long.

"Look at this picture, her first day of school."
"It's all black and white!" observed Tom, "That's so cool!"

"This one is Granny Eileen at the fair,
She had your cute freckles and your curly hair."

"This is their wedding!" said Tom, "look at that!"
"Your grandpa was wearing an elegant hat!"

"The guests look so funny with those frilly clothes!
Today's clothes are not as eccentric as those."

"Look at her running and having such fun!
That's from her holiday under the sun."

"Who is the baby she's holding?" asked Tom,
"That is your granny," she said. "That's my mom!"

"Great-Granny's smile is so big, can you see?
That's the same smile that you had holding me!"

"And this one was taken a few years ago,
She's giving a present to someone you know..."

"You?" exclaimed Tom, "That's you, am I right?"
Mom gave a giggle, "My boy is so bright!"

"So how about that one, the one on the wall?"
Mom replied, "That one's the best one of all."

"For that is the last time I saw her, you see,
That's why that photo is precious to me."

"Soon after that, I was told that she died.
I miss her so much," whispered mom teary-eyed.

But that's how it works. Not much can be done.
Life can be great, but we only get one.

And though it is true that she's no longer here,
My memories help me to feel her so near.

Each picture, each story, each hug that had been,
Will help us remember Great-Grandma Eileen.

The Do's and Don'ts of Talking with a Child about Death

- Children react differently depending on age. Preschool children mostly see death as temporary, reversible and impersonal. Between the ages of 5 and 9, most children are beginning to see that all living things eventually die and that death is final, but they do not relate it to themselves and they often think that that doesn't apply to them. From nine through to adolescence, children begin to understand that death is irreversible and that they too will die someday.

- A grieving child needs information that is clear and comprehensible for their development level. Use clear phrases, do not lie or use euphemisms like "The angels have taken her," or "She lives on the cloud now."

- Ask and answer questions. Be honest and straightforward, provide the facts, use books or other sources.

- Encourage expression, let them see your grief. Explain your feelings to your child.

- Create rituals. Creating rituals around remembering and honoring a loved one who died is another significant form of expression.

Your Free Gift

Thank you for buying my book!

Funny riddles for children

Visit my site to download it right now!

www.katemeltonbooks.com

Dear reader, you may also like these books!
Available on Amazon.com

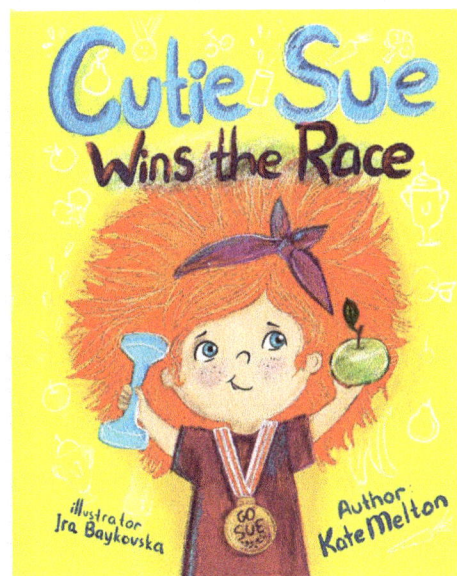

Cutie Sue Wins the Race
illustrator Ira Baykovska
Author: Kate Melton

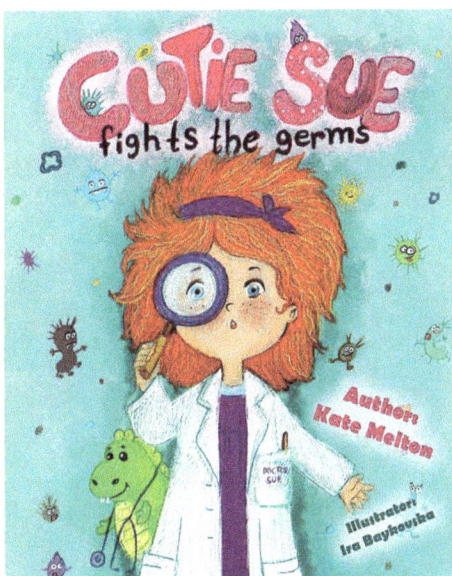

Cutie Sue fights the germs
Author: Kate Melton
Illustrator: Ira Baykovska

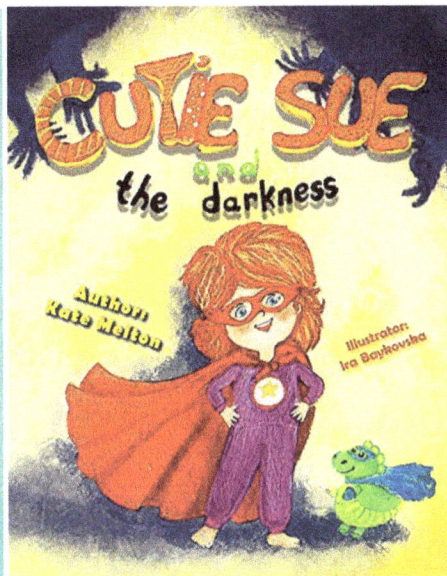

Cutie Sue and the darkness
Author: Kate Melton
Illustrator: Ira Baykovska

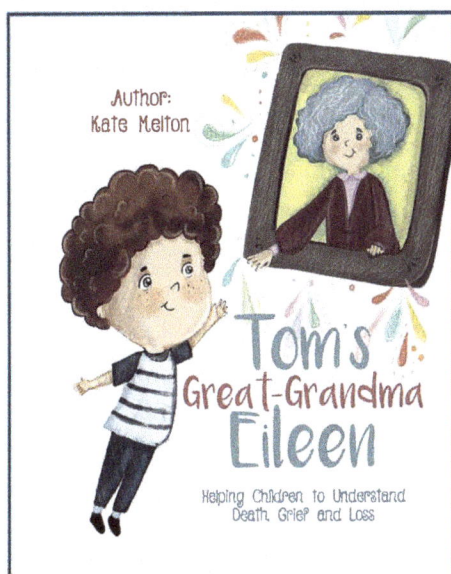

Author: Kate Melton
Tom's Great-Grandma Eileen
Helping Children to Understand Death, Grief and Loss

Little Dino Says "Please!"

Being a self-published author, I truly need readers' support. I would be extremely grateful if you could spend a minute to share your opinion about my book on Amazon.com!

www.ingramcontent.com/pod-product-compliance
Lightning Source LLC
Chambersburg PA
CBHW060946100426

42813CB00016B/2874